What People Are Saying About
Chicken Soup for the

"... If you liked James Herriot'[...] [...]or
the Pet Lover's Soul."

[...]ht
veterinarian and son of James Herriot

"The stories in *Chicken Soup for the Pet Lover's Soul* are powerful, heartwarming and full of life. Every story speaks to me of the special love we share with our pets. My dog Sheldon and I especially enjoyed this book."

Stephen R. Covey
author, *The Seven Habits of Highly Effective People*

"In our relationship to the world, the profoundest mystery of all is the power of love. *Chicken Soup for the Pet Lover's Soul* is about this mystery. It comes from and reveals the deepest recesses of the heart. This book is a joyful experience."

Roger A. Caras
author and president, ASPCA

"Thanks for honoring some of our most important friends on earth—our pets. *Chicken Soup for the Pet Lover's Soul* vividly illustrates how they enrich our lives in so many ways. I couldn't put the book down. You will love it!"

Monty Roberts
author, *The Man Who Listens to Horses*

"As a pet owner and lover, I know how important animals are to our sense of well-being and how deeply we love them. *Chicken Soup for the Pet Lover's Soul* is a perfect tribute to our special relationship with our pets."

Leeza Gibbons
executive producer and host, *Leeza*

"... Three things have sustained me through the worst and best of times: dogs, cats and chicken soup. Now all three of those lifesaving ingredients are combined in this collection of moving stories about the unique role that our beloved animals play in our lives. Keep the tissues handy. You'll need them."

Mordecai Siegal
author, *The Davis Book of Dogs*,
president, Dog Writer's Association of America, Inc.

"*Chicken Soup for the Pet Lover's Soul* is a happy lick and a friendly meow in your future—great reading for you and your pet in your 'Cocoon'!"

Faith Popcorn
consumer trend forecaster and founder, BrainReserve

"Simply the best feel-good collection of true stories from people who have loved and been loved by an animal companion."

Phyllis Levy
books editor, *Good Housekeeping* magazine

"*Chicken Soup for the Pet Lover's Soul* will help you heal, be happy and inspired and even save the world in the only way these miracles are possible: by sharing the spirit of hope and love that passes through all living things."

Michael Capuzzo
coauthor, *Cat Caught My Heart* and syndicated columnist, *Newsday*

"Finally a book I can read to my dogs! Seriously, *Chicken Soup for the Pet Lover's Soul* is a wonderful book—every story is a gem!"

Mathilde de Cagney
trainer of "Eddie" on *Frasier*

"These stories capture the true essence of the wonderful bond that exists between pets and their people. Every pet lover should have this book!"

Jeff Werber, D.V.M.
host of *Petcetera* on the Animal Planet Channel

"In a lifetime of loving animals, I have rarely come across anything as special as the stories in this book. If you've ever known the generous love of a companion animal, you'll cherish these stories."

Gina Spadafori
editorial director, Pet Care Forum on America Online,
author, *Dogs for Dummies*, coauthor, *Cats for Dummies*

"Take two stories and you'll feel better in the morning. Your spirits will be lifted by these true-life tales!"

Steve Dale
syndicated columnist, "My Pet World" and *PetLife* magazine
and host, WGN Radio's "Pet Central"

"Bravo! *Chicken Soup for the Pet Lover's Soul* is comforting and delicious."

Bea Arthur
actress